LOOK AT YOUR BODY
MUSCLES

STEVE PARKER
ILLUSTRATED BY IAN THOMPSON

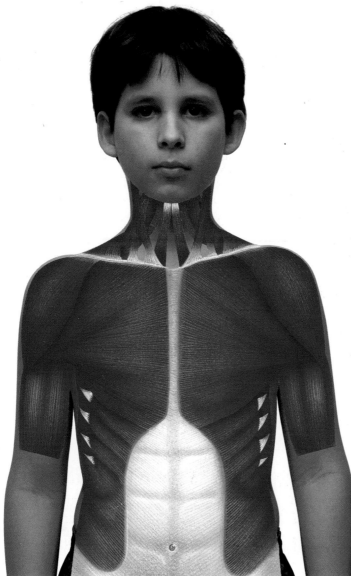

Copper Beech Books
Brookfield, Connecticut

*Designed and
produced by*
Aladdin Books Ltd
28 Percy Street
London W1P 0LD

*First published in
the United States
in 1997 by*
Copper Beech Books,
an imprint of
The Millbrook Press
2 Old New Milford
Road
Brookfield,
Connecticut 06804

Printed in Belgium

Editor
Jon Richards
Design
David West
Children's Book Design
Designer Flick Killerby
Illustrator
Ian Thompson
Picture Research
Brooks Krikler Research
Consultant
Dr. Rachel Levene
MB.BS, DCH, DRCOG

**Library of Congress
Cataloging-in-Publication Data**
Parker, Steve.
Muscles / Steve Parker ;
illustrated by Ian Thompson.
p. cm. — (Look at your body)
Includes index.
Summary: A comprehensive
look at the different types of
muscles in the human body and
how they function.
ISBN 0-7613-0612-9 (lib. bdg.)
1. Muscles—Juvenile literature.
[1. Muscles. 2. Muscular
system.]
I. Thompson, Ian, 1964- ill.
II. Title. III. Series.
QP321.P28 1997   97-8023
612.7′4—dc21   CIP AC

5 4 3 2 1

CONTENTS

INTRODUCTION

LOOK AT YOUR BODY! Wiggle your fingers, straighten your legs, and if there's a mirror nearby, make a funny face! Even these simple actions involve hundreds of your body's "movement devices" – muscles. Your body has about 640 of these and they work together in pairs and teams, to produce smooth and coordinated body motions. Muscles work in one simple way – by getting powerfully shorter, or contracting, according to instructions from your brain, sent out through your body's network of nerves. The complicated ways that muscles are arranged, and the ways they pull on the bones of the skeleton and other body parts, mean they can carry out a huge range of movements – from the tiniest blink of an eye to lifting a heavy weight with all your might.

MUSCLES *in* NATURE

THE LIVING WORLD is full of movement. Tree roots push through the soil, plant stems grow upward to the light, leaves unfurl, flower petals burst from buds, and microscopic organisms ooze through the mud in ponds and lakes.

These plant movements do not involve muscles, but almost every animal action depends on muscles and the tiny threadlike parts from which muscles are made called muscle fibers (*see* pages 10–11). This includes the movements of animals ranging from small and simple creatures, such as worms and insects, to big and complicated beasts, like humans, crocodiles, and whales.

HUMMING GNAT
The high-pitched hum of the gnat (above) is produced by the beating of its wings as it flies. The muscles used to flap the wings are ten times thinner than a human hair. They also work far faster than our own muscles, beating the wings about 1,000 times each second!

Exoskeleton   Joint   Muscles

Antenna

4

STRONG-ARMED APE

The gorilla (below) has almost the same number of muscles as you, arranged in much the same way. But its muscles are far bigger and stronger than yours, making up three fifths of its total body weight, while your muscles only make up two fifths of your weight.

However, most of the gorilla's head and face muscles are smaller and weaker than yours. So it cannot compete with the wide range of faces you can make (left).

SCURRYING ANT

Ants (below left) have six legs, and each leg is moved by about twelve tiny muscles. The muscles are attached to the inside of its hard outer casing, called the exoskeleton. As the ant runs, one muscle of a pair straightens or extends the joint, while its partner bends or flexes the joint (left). Together these teams of muscles move the leg forward and back, about 20 times each second. Inside the ant's antennae, or feelers, are similar, yet even smaller, muscles!

WIGGLING WORM

Even the humble earthworm (below) has muscles! There are two main sets of muscles along the worm's body. One set runs lengthwise, and when they contract, the body becomes shorter and fatter. The other set is circular, and when they contract, the body becomes longer and thinner.

HUMAN MUSCLES

SOME OF YOUR MUSCLES are arranged in identical sets on either side of your body. These teams of muscles are the ones that give you your full range of movements, from raising your eyebrows to swinging your legs. They are also responsible for giving your body the shape it has – with a little help from some pads of fat. Because most of them are fixed to the bones of your skeleton, they are called skeletal muscles.

The body also has two other types of muscle tissue – cardiac and smooth muscle. Cardiac muscle is found in the heart, while smooth is found in your internal organs (*see* pages 20–21).

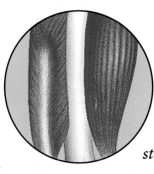

SKELETAL MUSCLE
Skeletal muscle is usually attached to bones. It can be controlled by conscious decisions. The tiny fibers in skeletal muscle form a pattern of narrow bands, so it is also known as striped muscle.

SMOOTH MUSCLE
This muscle tissue is found in the walls of internal organs. It performs many roles that you are not aware of, such as pushing food around your guts.

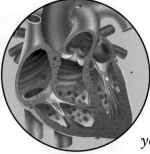

CARDIAC MUSCLE
This type of muscle tissue makes up the thick walls of the heart. Cardiac muscle has a specialized structure that means it should never fatigue, or get tired, pumping blood around your body even when you sleep.

6

1

2

3

4

5

6

7

UNDER THE SKIN

The skeletal muscles of the body are basically arranged in two layers. The superficial layer (shown below) is the layer of muscle nearest the skin. Below this lies the deep layer of muscles.

GUIDE TO THE MAJOR BODY MUSCLES
The numbers refer to the major muscles of the body (below left).

1 Neck muscles – including sternocleidomastoid
2 Shoulder muscles – including trapezius
3 Rear arm muscles – including triceps
4 Back muscles – including latissimus dorsi
5 Buttocks – including gluteus maximus
6 Rear thigh muscles – including hamstrings
7 Calf muscles – including gastrocnemius

8 Chest muscles – including pectoralis major
9 Front arm muscles – including biceps
10 Stomach muscles – including abdominals
11 Inner leg muscles – including adductors
12 Front of the thigh muscles – including sartorius
13 Shin muscles – including the tibialis anterior

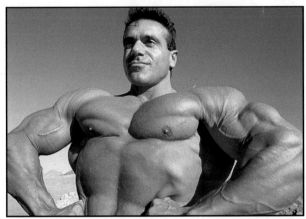

7

MUSCLES AND BODY SHAPE

The basic shape of your body is determined by the bones of your skeleton. Your height and number of muscles cannot be altered by exercise. But the relative sizes and shapes of muscles can.

A person who does plenty of bodybuilding activity develops bulging muscles (above). These muscles give explosive but short-term power. On the other hand, a long-distance runner (right) has a lighter body, but also very efficient lungs and leg muscles, and a strong heart to give extra stamina. For a more standard body shape (left), deposits of fat also contribute to the outline.

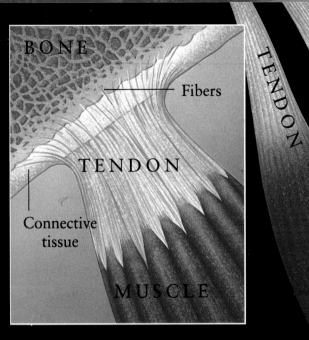

BONE

Fibers

TENDON

Connective
tissue

MUSCLE

TENDON

TENDON

TENDONS

These ropelike parts, made of tough and stringy fibers, taper from the narrow end, or head, of the muscle. Their other ends, embedded firmly in the bone, attach the muscle (left).

Blood vessel

MUSCLE BELLY

ANATOMY OF MUSCLES

Whatever their size or shape, all skeletal or voluntary muscles have the same basic structure (right). The main bulk of the muscle, which is called the belly, is the part that contracts, or gets shorter. At either end are the tendons that fix the muscle in place (see above).

The shape of the belly affects the strength and range of movement of a muscle. The longer the muscle, the more it can contract. As a result, it can move a body part over a greater distance. For example, the muscles of the leg have long bellies and can bend the leg completely, while the short jaw muscles can only move a small amount.

Nerve

The body's longest, thickest, and strongest tendon is the Achilles' tendon (*left*), just above the heel. It links the calf muscle to the back of the heel bone, the calcaneus. It comes under strain as the calf muscle contracts and pulls the heel up, to point the foot. The Achilles' tendon is sometimes torn or injured, especially when the foot is twisted one way and the body and leg jerk the other way during some sports.

NERVES

Motor nerves carry messages from the brain to your muscles, telling them when to contract and by how much (see pages 22–23). Other nerves relay messages back to the brain. These tell the brain how the movement is going, as well as the position of the body part, and allow you to fine-tune the movement.

8

All SHAPES AND SIZES

IN ORDER TO DO THEIR JOB PROPERLY, muscles must have certain characteristics. Their shape and size must match the job they are to do – your body has hundreds of differently shaped muscles, each with a specific role. For example, larger muscles are needed where a great force is required, while small muscles are used for delicate operations.

Muscles also need strong connective cords to transfer their force to the bones. These come in the form of tendons, found at either end of the muscle. Finally, like any other body part, every muscle also has its own supply systems in the form of blood vessels and nerves.

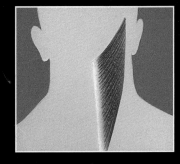

Strap muscle

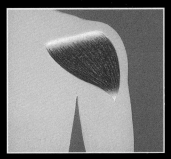

Triangular muscle

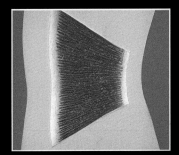

Sheet muscle

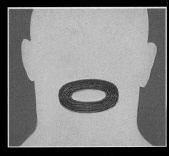

Sphincter muscle

BLOOD SUPPLY
Blood brings nutrients to the muscles. The blood vessels branch throughout a muscle to supply all its parts. During exercise, muscles need more nutrients, so the vessels widen and the heart pumps faster.

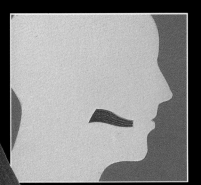

MUSCLE SHAPES
Muscles have several basic shapes. For example, muscle sheets, such as the abdominals in your stomach region, form layers over body parts. These muscles can be tensed to form a stiff protective "wall." A sphincter is a ring or circle of muscle, such as the orbicularis oris around your mouth. When it contracts, the hole or passage within it gets smaller or closes completely. Other muscle shapes include triangular, such as the deltoid in your shoulder and strap, such as the splenius capitis in your neck (right).

MUSCLE LENGTHS
A straplike muscle may be short, like the risorius major in the cheek (above).This pulls the corner of the mouth sideways into a grin (see pages 14–15). Alternatively, it may be long, such as the flexor digitalis in the forearm (right). This has long tendons that run through the wrist. As its name suggests, this muscle flexes the digits – bends the fingers.

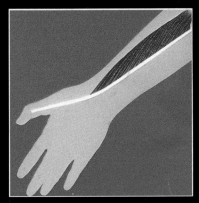

TENDON

9

Blood vessels

Muscle

Muscle
fascicle

Epimysium

MUSCLE BULK
*The bundles of
muscle fascicles are
tightly packed to fill
the belly of each
muscle. In a cross-
section of skeletal
muscle, these bundles
are clearly visible under
a microscope (left).*

Once a person has
died, the actin and
myosin strands in muscles
no longer have fresh energy
supplies to contract or relax.
They become "locked" together.
This makes the muscle hard
and rigid, a condition called
rigor mortis. This becomes
apparent about 6 hours after
death and begins to fade after
about 36 hours, as the proteins
deteriorate.

INSIDE *a* MUSCLE

LIKE MOST BODY PARTS, a muscle has a tough and flexible outer covering of connective tissue, called the muscle sheath, or epimysium. Beneath this, the muscle is made up of increasingly smaller and smaller parts.

Making up most of the muscle's bulk are the muscle fascicles, bundles of tightly packed muscle cells, called muscle fibers. Each muscle fiber is about the thickness of a human hair. Muscle fibers are made up of smaller threadlike structures called fibrils and inside these are hundreds of microscopic muscle filaments.

MUSCLE FILAMENTS
These form the smallest part of the muscle cell. They are, in fact thin strands of protein (below). There are two types of muscle filaments. The thicker strand is called myosin, and the thinner strand, called actin. It is these tiny strands that slide over each other, causing the muscle to contract. Although each strand only moves a small distance, the combined movement of millions of these tiny strands can result in a large muscle movement.

11

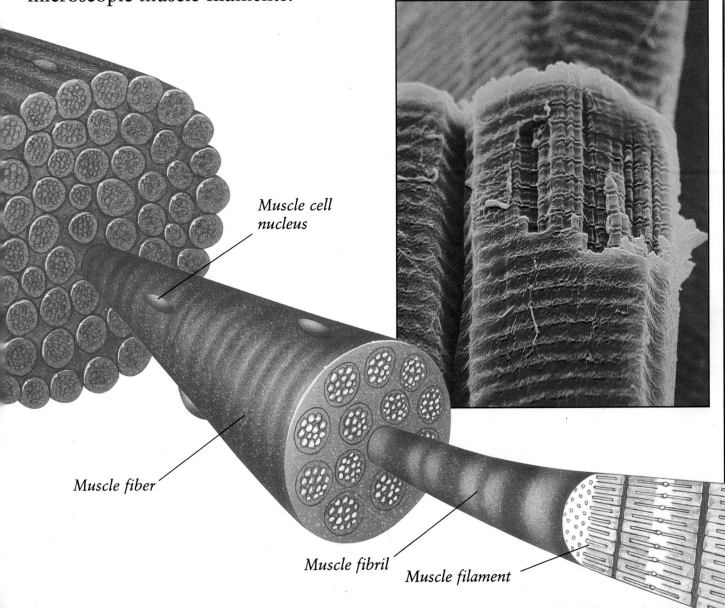

Muscle cell nucleus

Muscle fiber

Muscle fibril

Muscle filament

How MUSCLES WORK

The simplest joints have two movements – bending and straightening. However, muscles that move them can only exert a pulling force. As a result, muscles must work in opposing teams to create the full range of movement – one set pulls to bend the joint and the other pulls to straighten it (*see below*). This pulling action is achieved by the movement of the tiny actin and myosin muscle filaments.

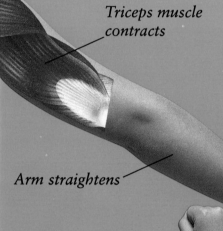

Triceps muscle contracts

Arm straightens

MUSCLE PARTNERS
Many muscles are arranged as opposing partners, or antagonistic pairs – as for example, the calf and shin muscles contract to point and raise the foot (right).

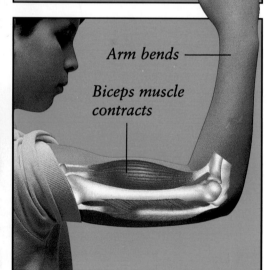

Arm bends

Biceps muscle contracts

BULGING BICEPS
As with the leg, the arm has two opposing muscles to move it – the biceps and triceps (above).

SHIN MUSCLE RELAXES

CALF MUSCLE CONTRACTS

FOOT IS POINTED

12

THE MOBILE THUMB

The thumb is an example of a complicated joint. Its bones are pulled by the tendons of seven main muscles, almost equally spaced around its sides (below). Working as a team, they contract or relax by precise amounts, and can pull the thumb in any direction – you can wave its tip around in a circle.

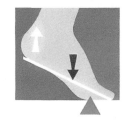

LEVERS

Many muscles move body parts using the lever principle. This is when a lever, e.g. a bone, moves a load (1, above), e.g. the weight of the body, by applying a force from a contracting muscle (2) around a pivot (3), e.g. a joint. In mechanics, there are three basic types of levers, and the body has examples of all of them (above and below).

SHIN MUSCLE CONTRACTS

CALF MUSCLE RELAXES

13

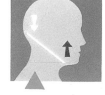

PULLING POWER

When a muscle contracts, the tiny actin muscle filaments slide along the myosin muscle filaments (above), effectively shortening the length of the whole muscle. This movement is achieved by special chemical links, called cross-bridges, which form between the actin and myosin filaments and pull them past each other. The action is very similar to people pulling hand-over-hand on a rope. When a muscle relaxes, the cross-bridges break, allowing the muscle filaments to slide apart (below).

Actin filament   Myosin filament

FOOT IS RAISED

The FACE AND HEAD

FROWN
Muscles on each side of your mouth depress, or pull down, the corner of your lips to make a frown (below).

IT'S OFFICIAL – it is easier to grin than to grimace. Smiling uses about 20 facial muscles, while frowning uses over 40. Most of the muscles in your head are used to create the wide range of facial expressions you can produce. These facial muscles are small to produce the delicate movements needed. There are also small muscles involved in moving your eyes around. Your head, too, has powerful muscles. These include the muscles in your jaw that help you bite, as well as the strong muscles in your neck.

EYE MUSCLES
Around the eyeball are six small, strap-shaped muscles, like pieces of elastic (right). They are attached to the eye's outer sheath at the front and to the rear of the eye socket. Working in precise teams, they swivel and move the eyeball within its socket, or orbit. This means you can look

FACIAL EXPRESSIONS
The eyebrow needs to be raised only slightly, by a muscle in the forehead, to produce a quizzical or surprised look. However, if another muscle pulls it inward and down, the expression becomes perplexed or even annoyed. Most people learn to control their facial muscles with great precision to create a whole range of facial expressions (left).

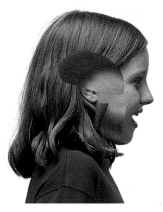

BITING AND CHEWING

In order to chew food thoroughly while eating, the lower jaw and teeth are pulled up against the upper jaw with great force. This is carried out mainly by two pairs of large and powerful muscles situated on either side of your head (left). These are the temporalis, found in the region of each temple, just behind the eyes, and the masseter, which is found just behind either cheek.

Food is also moved around and massaged by your very flexible tongue (above right). Made up almost entirely of muscle, the tongue can be manipulated into a wide range of shapes to help you eat, drink, speak, and even whistle.

SMILE

A muscle, running from the cheek bone to the angle of the lip, pulls the corner of the mouth up and out. It is aided by other muscles, closer to the middle of the mouth and toward the side (below).

GUIDE TO THE MUSCLES OF THE HEAD

Listed below are the major muscles of the face, head, and neck, with the actions they produce.

1 *Raises eyebrows (as with a look of surprise) – frontalis*

2 *Tilts the head to either side and rotates the head (as with looking from side to side) – sternocleidomastoid*

3 *Pulls out part of lower lip and tenses the skin of the neck – platysma*

4 *Widens the nasal openings (as in deep breathing) – nasalis*

5 *Closes the eyelid, both gently (as in winking) and tightly (as against bright light) – orbicularis oculi*

6 *Lifts the jaw to close the mouth – masseter*

7 *Pulls the scalp back – occipitalis*

8 *Pulls back the head, tilts the head to one side, and rotates the head – splenius capitis*

The TORSO

T he central part of the human body, called the torso, has several sets of muscles. Those for the neck extend up into the skull and head. Muscles that move the upper arm are found in the region of the shoulders and chest. Around the stomach, sheets of muscles form walls protecting the digestive system. Also, deep inside your chest lie the sets of muscles that help you to breathe and keep you alive.

BENDING
The large, sheetlike muscles in the front stomach region, the abdominals, help to bend the torso forward (above). A complex series of muscles along the side of the backbone, including the external obliques, contract to bend the torso to one side (below).

GUIDE TO THE MUSCLES OF THE FRONT OF THE TORSO
Listed below are the major muscles of the front of the torso and the actions they produce.

1 Tilts the head to the side and turns the head to look over either shoulder – sternocleidomastoid
2 Raises, pulls back, and rotates the shoulder blades – trapezius
3 Pulls the arm forward and rotates the shoulder blade – pectoralis major
4 Pulls down, rotates, and pulls back each of the shoulder blades – latissimus dorsi
5 Tilts the body to the side – External obliques
6 Bends the body forward -- Abdominals

16

Intercostal muscle

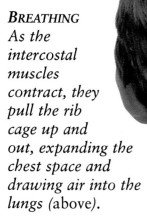

MUSCLES FOR BREATHING

The movements of breathing depend on two main sets of muscles. One is a dome-shaped sheet, the diaphragm, found in the base of the chest, under the lungs. The other is the intercostal group of muscles (*left*), which lie between each of the ribs.

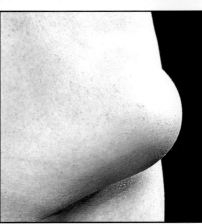

BREATHING
As the intercostal muscles contract, they pull the rib cage up and out, expanding the chest space and drawing air into the lungs (*above*).

Various parts of the body, especially the stomach region, are covered with sheets of muscle that surround softer parts within, such as the intestines. Occasionally, one of these muscles may develop a weakness. This allows the soft tissue within to poke through and form a bulge under the skin, which is called a hernia (*above*). If this causes problems, it can be pushed back in through the area of weakness during an operation, and the weak area sewn up.

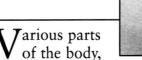

17

GUIDE TO THE MUSCLES OF THE BACK OF THE TORSO
Listed below are the major muscles of the back of the torso and the movements they produce.

1 Tilts the head to the side and turns the head to look over either shoulder – sternocleidomastoid

2 Raises, pulls back, and rotates the shoulder blades – trapezius

3 Rotates the arms – infraspinatus

4 Rotates the arms – teres minor

5 Pulls back and rotates the arms – teres major

6 Lowers, rotates, and pulls back each of the shoulder blades – latissimus dorsi

The ARMS AND LEGS

THE LARGER AND STRONGER muscles that move your arms and legs are found in your shoulders and hips. In comparison, the muscles actually found in your limbs are quite small. This gives less weight to the limbs, and so decreases the energy needed to make them move, especially when performing quick actions, such as running.

As well as the strong movements of lifting, walking, and running, your limbs perform small, delicate, but no less important actions. Without the precise movements of your fingers you would not be able to turn the pages of this book!

GUIDE TO THE MUSCLES OF THE UPPER AND LOWER ARM
Listed below are the major muscles found in the upper and lower arm and the movements they produce.

1 *Raises and rotates the upper arm – deltoid*

2 *Straightens and extends the lower arm – triceps*

3 *Flexes and rotates the elbow to bend the arm – biceps*

4 *Bends back the wrist – extensors*

5 *Flexes the elbow to bend the arm – brachioradialis*

6 *Flexes and pulls the wrist forward – flexors*

The condition known as tennis elbow results from the straining and swelling of some of the muscles and tendons in the forearm. This straining is usually caused by a decay of some of the tendons that run up and down your arm.

Tendon

Tennis elbow commonly affects people who regularly stretch their arms backward, while pushing against a resistance. This action is very similar to playing a tennis backhand (*below*), hence the name of the condition.

LEG MUSCLES
The muscles in your legs are always adjusting to keep your center of gravity acting through your hips, knees, and ankles (below), helping you to stay upright. Alternatively, they also give you the power to jump up and down, or to walk and run.

THE HANDS
About 20 strong, cordlike tendons pass through the wrist from the long muscles in the forearm, to the bones of the palm and fingers. Those tendons on the back or outside of the wrist come from extensor muscles. They extend or straighten the fingers. Those on the wrist's inside come from flexor muscles and they bend or curl the fingers. In addition there are smaller muscles alongside the palm and finger bones themselves – the interossei and lumbricals. These help to give the finger control that allows you to carry out many delicate activities, such as playing the piano (above).

GUIDE TO THE MUSCLES OF THE UPPER AND LOWER LEG
Listed below are the major muscles found in the upper and lower leg.

1 Pulls back the leg and rotates the hip – gluteus maximus

2 Pulls back the leg and flexes the knee to bend the lower leg – hamstrings

3 Pulls the leg into the body and extends and rotates the hip – adductors

4 Pulls the leg forward, flexes the hip, and extends the knee – rectus femoris

5 Pulls on the ankle to point the foot – gastrocnemius

6 Helps to steady the legs while standing – soleus

7 Flexes the ankle joint to pull the feet up – tibialis anterior

19

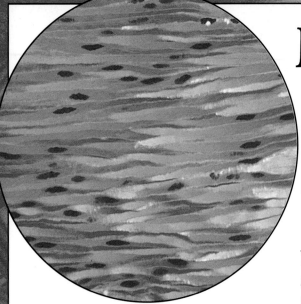

SMOOTH MUSCLE
Under the microscope, smooth muscle (above) lacks the bands that make up skeletal, or striped, muscle. This is because its fibers are shorter and arranged in a random fashion. It is known as smooth muscle.

MUSCLES *on the* INSIDE

THERE ARE TWO TYPES of muscles found deep inside your body – smooth and cardiac muscle. Cardiac muscle is only found in the walls of the heart, pushing blood out into the arteries.

Smooth muscles are found in the walls of your internal organs, such as the digestive and respiratory systems. They are also found in some of the walls of your blood vessels, helping to control the flow of blood around your body.

1 RESPIRATORY SYSTEM
There are layers of smooth muscle in the walls of the branching airways in the chest, including the trachea, or windpipe, the main airways or bronchi in each lung, and especially in the smaller, thinner airways, called bronchioles.

2 DIGESTIVE SYSTEM
Layers of smooth muscle are found in the digestive system. There are usually two layers, one running around the tube and one running along it. These layers contract to push the food along the gut in an action called peristalsis (below).

URINARY SYSTEM
In the urinary system, urine is squeezed from the kidneys by waves of peristalsis (see above right) along tubes called ureters and down to the bladder.

REPRODUCTIVE SYSTEM
In the female reproductive system, waves of peristalsis (see above) in the fallopian tubes massage a ripe egg from the ovary, or egg-producing gland, toward the uterus, or womb.

20

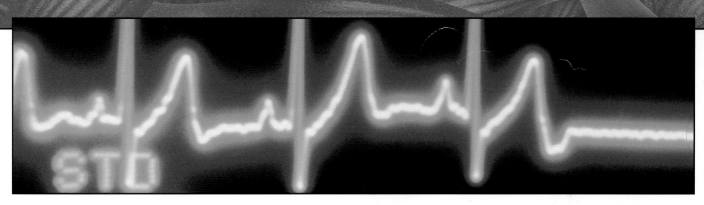

NEVER-ENDING RHYTHM

With each heartbeat, blood is let into the two atria (1, right). Valves then open to let blood into the ventricles (2). From here it is pumped into the arteries (3), and more blood is let into the atria (4). Doctors can check your heart by detecting the electrical currents made by the muscles. This is shown on an electrocardiogram (ECG, above).

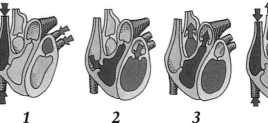

1   2   3   4

Right atrium

Left atrium

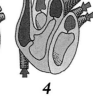

CARDIAC MUSCLE

Under the microscope this has a slightly striped appearance, like skeletal muscle. But the stripes are less regular and some may be Y-shaped or branched (left).

THE HEART

The two upper chambers of the heart, the atria, have very thin walls, and little cardiac muscle (left). The larger chambers of the heart, the ventricles, have thick walls of cardiac muscle. They need this muscle to force blood into the arteries under pressure.

Valve

5

Right ventricle

Left ventricle

CIRCULATORY SYSTEM

Arteries have smooth muscles in their walls, with the fibers arranged around the blood vessel. As they contract, they narrow the space for blood to flow through. This slows the flow and causes pressure to build up. It is one of the brain's ways of controlling blood pressure. Also, contraction of smooth muscle in the artery supplying an organ controls the blood supply to that organ.

In some forms of heart disease, the heart stops beating (cardiac arrest), or it beats too fast, in an ineffective manner (fibrillation). To correct this, doctors may send an electrical current through the heart, using a defibrillator, with electrodes placed on the chest (*right*). This may "shock" the muscle of the heart back into its regular beat.

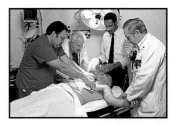

19
18
17
16
15
14
13
12
11
10
9
8
7
6
5
4
3
2
1

WEIRD BODY
If the shape of your body reflected the area of the motor cortex given to each part then you would look very strange. You would have huge hands and feet and a large head while your body, arms, and legs would be very small (right).

1
2
3

MOVEMENT CENTERS
The two movement centers in the brain are known as the motor cortexes. These are two strips that run along the brain's surface, called the cerebral cortex. Each movement center can be divided into segments, with each segment controlling the movement of a specific body part.

The diagram (above) shows which segments of the motor cortex control which body parts.
1 Swallowing, 2 Tongue, 3 Jaw, 4 Lips, 5 Face, 6 Eyelid and eyeball, 7 Brow, 8 Neck, 9 Thumb, 10, 11, and 12 Fingers, 13 Hand, 14 Wrist, 15 Elbow, 16 Shoulder, 17 Trunk, 18 Hip, 19 Knee, 20 Ankle, 21 Toes.

22

BALANCE
Balance is an ongoing process involving nerve signals from many sense organs. The brain continuously analyzes these signals and sends out signals to adjust the muscles and keep you standing upright.

Under CONTROL

ALL MUSCLES are controlled by the brain. They need nerve signals from the brain, in the form of tiny electrical pulses traveling along motor nerves. These pulses act as signals, telling the muscle when, and by how much, to contract. Skeletal muscles are controlled from parts that lie across the top of the brain, called the movement centers, or motor cortexes. Smooth muscles are controlled from deep within the brain, where many other vital life processes are controlled. The signals to the smooth muscles are sent without you having to make a conscious decision.

MAKING A MUSCLE MOVE
1 The motor cortex starts a series of electrical nerve signals, called the central motor program. These signals will make the appropriate muscles contract to carry out the movement.
2 Some signals pass through the cerebellum, found at the rear of the brain. This "fine-tunes" the movement and coordinates with other body movements.
3 The signals pass down the spinal cord, and out along motor nerves, to the intended muscle.
4 Stretch and tension sensors in the muscle send signals back to areas in the brain, informing them how the movement is progressing.

FROM SPINE TO MUSCLE
Nerve signals pass from the spine along nerve branches toward their intended muscle (right). These nerves end at a motor end plate (below). Here the signal is passed across a tiny gap, called a synapse, to the muscle which then starts to contract in response to the signal.

23

4

MUSCLES *for* STRENGTH

EVERYONE HAS ABOUT THE SAME NUMBER of skeletal muscles. Exercise cannot increase the number of muscles, but it can increase the bulk of a muscle. There are two main kinds of exercise, anaerobic and aerobic. In anaerobic exercise, the muscles are active for only a brief period – in quick, explosive actions such as weightlifting, shot-putting, or sprinting. Anaerobic exercise may build muscle bulk and strength, but does not contribute much to body fitness, compared to aerobic exercise (*see* page 26).

(*see* page 26)

24

INTENSE EXERCISE
Intensive weight-training builds up the bulk of a muscle by increasing the number of actin and myosin filaments in each muscle fiber. This has the effect of increasing the diameter and strength of each muscle.

Anabolic steroids are artificially made steroid chemicals that stimulate the growth of some body tissues, including muscle. However, their use in sports is illegal. Some competitors who rely on appearance, such as bodybuilders, or short-term power, such as sprinters, have used them to increase muscle bulk.

MUSCLE EFFICIENCY

Greater activity and exercise increases the size of muscles. This is called muscular hypertrophy. It also causes the muscle to use its supplies of oxygen and energy more efficiently. Some highly trained athletes can convert as much as 40% of the energy they are supplied with into movement. Alternatively, lack of exercise decreases muscle bulk and may cause a body to become thinner (left). This is called muscular atrophy. The muscles become floppy, weak, and less efficient. They may only be able to convert as little as 10% of the energy they are supplied with into movement.

SHORT-TERM POWER

Explosive anaerobic exercise, such as intensive sprinting (above), can only occur for short periods of time. With very intense exercise, the lungs take in insufficient oxygen for the muscles. As a result, the muscles produce more waste products, such as lactic acid. If these waste products build up without resting the muscles, they can cause muscle fatigue (below), and even cramping (see page 27).

220

MUSCLES *for* FITNESS

WHILE ANAEROBIC EXERCISE makes your muscles bigger and stronger (*see* pages 24–25), aerobic exercise makes them fitter. They become more efficient at using supplies of sugar and oxygen and are able to work consistently for much longer periods without getting tired. Every muscle, including your heart, can benefit from moderate amounts of aerobic exercise. But be careful, too much exercise can cause problems.

SLOWER HEART
The heart of a fit person will beat slower than that of an unfit one. Their pulse rate may be over 40% lower!

AEROBIC EXERCISE
Aerobic exercise includes any activity that makes the heart and lungs work faster and harder for at least 15–20 minutes. In this time, the muscles as well as the heart, circulatory, and respiratory systems are well exercised. It also increases blood flow that carries away waste. Regular and steady swimming (above), jogging, or playing ballgames all have beneficial aerobic effects.

A cramp is an uncontrolled contraction or spasm of a muscle. The muscle becomes hard and rigid, exerts a strong pulling force, and feels tense, knotted, and painful. There are various causes and types of cramps. It happens occasionally to a muscle that has not been active for some time and is then used strenuously, or to a muscle that has been squashed or distorted by sitting or lying on it. The cramp may be caused by continuous, uncoordinated bursts of signals from the nerve controlling the muscle, or a buildup of chemical waste products within the muscle. The usual remedy is to massage and stretch the muscle firmly (*left*).

EXHAUSTION

Skeletal muscles cannot work for extremely long periods. Strenuous exercise that uses one main group of muscles for too long can cause problems. The lungs may not be able to absorb enough oxygen, and the heart may not be able to supply enough blood to these muscles. The result can be severe stress and exhaustion (above). In extreme conditions, some body processes almost shut down, so that other, more vital processes, such as supplying blood to the brain, can continue.

27

ENERGY AND MUSCLES

The body's main energy source of blood sugar, or glucose, from food is carried by the blood to all cells. Inside a cell, glucose is broken down to release its energy, which the cell uses for its life processes. For example, muscle cells use energy to contract. The breakdown of glucose happens in tiny mitochondria found in each cell (above). The more mitochondria, the more glucose can be converted, giving more available energy. Aerobic exercise increases the number of mitochondria in each muscle cell.

DISEASES *and* INJURIES

USCLE TISSUE is relatively unaffected by disease compared to other body tissues. Inherited (genetic) and degenerative diseases are relatively uncommon, though some, such as the various forms of muscular dystrophy, are well known and the subject of intense medical research.

However, compared to other body tissues, skeletal muscles are relatively prone to stress and injury, including tears, strains, and even paralysis.

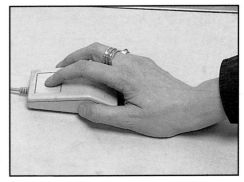

RSI
If the same action is repeated frequently, then the muscles, tendons, joints, and other parts involved may become stiff and painful, a condition known as repetitive strain injury, or RSI.

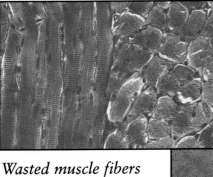

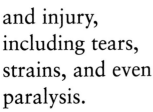

Wasted muscle fibers (right) appear small under a microscope. Compare them with normal fibers (above).

The latest artificial limbs (*left*) can move at the wearer's will, mimicking the actions of lost limbs and muscles. The muscle-type motion is caused by small electric motors linked to gears or cables that pull on the limb's parts. The mechanisms are arranged in opposing or antagonistic pairs, like real muscles. The wearer can control the movement by tensing the muscles remaining in the limb stump. Sensors in the artificial limb detect the tiny electrical signals from the muscles, and activate the servos. The artificial limb is called a myoelectric prosthesis.

MUSCLE WASTING
Muscular dystrophies are a group of disorders in which the muscle tissue becomes weak and gradually wastes away (above). The best-known is Duchenne muscular dystrophy, which tends to affect boys by the age of three. The wasted muscles mean that keeping body posture and moving becomes difficult. Weakened breathing muscles mean that chest infections also become more likely.

PARALYSIS

Paralysis is usually caused by damage to the motor nerves, the brain, or the spine. The extent of the paralysis depends on the site of the damage. Paraplegia (which affects both legs, 1, below) is caused by damage to the lower spine. Hemiplegia (which affects an arm and leg on one side, 2) is caused by damage to the brain, while quadriplegia (which affects both arms and legs, 3) is caused by damage to the neck.

PULLED MUSCLE

A muscle subjected to excessive pull or strain, such as during a violent movement while playing a sport, may have some of its fibers ruptured or even torn.

This causes the natural repair reaction of inflammation and swelling, and perhaps bleeding in the muscle tissue. This bleeding in the muscle can lead to excessive bruising around the site of the injury (above). The muscle becomes painful for a few hours after the injury, then aches for a few days. However, the damage is usually repaired naturally by the body.

TORN TENDON

If a muscle pulls too hard on its bone, the tendon linking the two may tear or even sever. This means the muscle can no longer pull the bone, so in addition to pain, there is a loss of movement.

SWOLLEN TENDONS

Sometimes tendons may swell, causing pain (right). This can be caused by too much exercise or even ill-fitting shoes.

KNOW YOUR BODY!

A NORMAL PERSON *has 640 muscles.*
These reach their maximum size, in
normal growth, by 20–25 years of
age. At this age nearly two fifths of
your body weight is made up from
muscle tissue (although this fraction
can increase with muscle-building exercise
– see pages 24–25). However, you get older, the amount
of muscle tissue in your
body decreases and is
partly replaced by fatty
tissue. By the time your
body gets to the age of
80, nearly half of this
maximum muscle mass
is lost (above).

THE EYE'S *fine*
movements are
controlled by tiny
straplike muscles
(above). Each nerve
fiber to the eye controls
only 12 muscle fibers,
allowing very delicate
movements – normally
one nerve fiber would
control thousands of
muscle fibers.

ASTRONAUTS *who*
spend longer than 90
days in space (left) lose
up to 20% of their leg
strength through
disuse. To combat this,
space stations have
exercise machines to
keep astronauts fit.

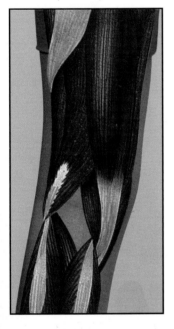

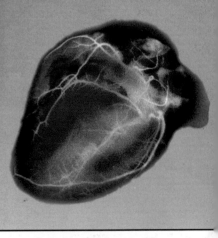

THE SHORTEST MUSCLE *is*
the stapedius, which is
0.2 in (0.5 cm) long and is found deep within
the ear (below), while the longest is the
sartorius in the thigh, which can be 12 in
(30 cm) long. The legs also have the longest
tendons, including those in the rear of your
thigh (above). The largest muscle is the gluteus
maximus in the buttock and the largest group
of muscles is the quadriceps
femoris in the leg. The
strongest muscles in your body,
relative to their size, are the
masseter muscles in your jaw.

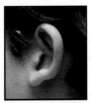

THE HEART *of a*
person (right) is
about the size of a
fist and weighs, on
average, 0.7 lbs
(0.3 kg). Compare
this with the heart
of a whale, which
is the size of a
small family car. A human heart will beat about
70 times a minute, 100,000 beats a day, and
about 2.5 billion times during a 70-year lifespan.

GLOSSARY

Actin – A protein that makes up some of the muscle filaments.

Aerobic respiration – The production of energy that involves oxygen.

Anaerobic respiration – The production of energy that does not involve the use of oxygen.

Antagonistic pairs – Two muscles or muscle teams that oppose the movement of each other. When one contracts, the other must relax to allow the joint to either bend or straighten.

Bone – The hard tissue that forms your skeleton. It is made up of collagen fibers, mineral crystals, and ground substance. It is also called osseous tissue.

Cardiac muscle – This is a specialized form of muscle tissue that is found only in the walls of the heart.

Center of gravity – The point through which the weight of the body is said to act. In you, this is found between the hips.

Cross-bridges – The chemical links that form between muscle filaments and pull them past each other, causing a muscle to contract.

Electrocardiogram (ECG) – A recording that measures the electrical waves of the heart muscle.

Exoskeleton – The tough skeleton found on the outside of some animals.

Intercostal muscles – The muscles found between the ribs which contract to lift the rib cage.

Joints – The points where two or more bones meet.

Lungs – A pair of organs that are the sites of oxygen absorption. They are found in the chest.

Muscle belly – The fleshy center of a muscle, often found at its widest part.

Muscle fascicles – Bundles of muscle fibers.

Muscle fibers – The cells of a muscle, so called because they look more like a fiber than a typical cell.

Muscle fibrils – The tiny threadlike parts that make up a muscle fiber.

Muscle filaments – The microscopic protein strands, either actin or myosin, that make up a muscle fibril.

Muscles – A collection of muscle fibers that can contract or relax to move body parts.

Myosin – A protein that makes up some of the muscle filaments.

Rigor mortis – The stiffening of the body that occurs several hours after a person has died.

Skeletal muscle – The muscle tissue that is attached to the skeleton and can contract voluntarily – also called voluntary muscle. It is also known as striped muscle because the tiny filaments are arranged in bands that can be seen under a microscope.

Smooth muscle – The muscle tissue that is found in the walls of the internal organs, such as the stomach. It is called smooth muscle because it lacks the bands seen in skeletal, or striped, muscle.

Sphincter – A circular muscle that helps keep an opening or tubular structure closed, such as the orbicularis oris around the mouth.

Tendon – A strong cord of stringlike fibers that attaches a muscle to a bone.

Torso – The main part of your body, excluding the head, arms, and legs.

INDEX

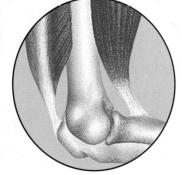

Photo credits:
Abbreviations: t-top, m-middle, b-bottom, r-right, l-left

All the photographs in this book are by Roger Vlitos except the
following pages;
Front cover ml, 7tl, 8m, 10b, 11, 17tr, 18t, 19b, 20t, 21 all, 23b,
27b, 28m & b, 29mr & b & 30br – Science Photo Library. 3tl,
7ml & bl, 19t, 24, 25tr & m, 26b, 26–27, 27tl & tr – Frank
Spooner Pictures. 30m – NASA.

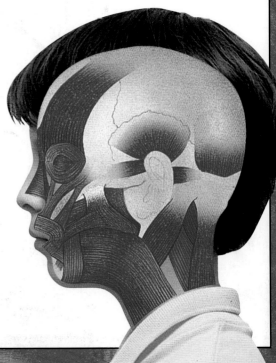